To Tony

road kill is a journey into the secret lives of our native animals. It starts in town, travels through suburbia, onto country roads and then out into the woods where fact and myth may mingle

very best wishes
David

Nadia x

+ thanks for "the fishing officer" + the barking mad gaffer!

Parole Parlates May 13

The Secret Fox

This is the secret fox
Whose track crossed your path, and crossed it again
Between your arriving and your leaving.

This is the secret fox
Whose sudden tail-flicker flash of flame
Lifted the sun through the arms of the trees.

This is the secret fox
Whose rasp of bark woke you from the dream voice
Whose words you are already forgetting.

This is the secret fox
Whose eyes gleam, who grins in the dark
From the den in the hidden corner of the bedroom.

This is the secret fox
Who leaves his ragged, smashed skin on the roadside
And comes to you shining with bones, with stars.

Suburban nights

The hedgehog grunts.
His nose shrew-snuffles.
Dead slugs. Green pellets.
He crunches and swallows.

Hunting out his body weight
in insects every night,
his journeying frustrated
by flat-panelled hedgerows.

In his search for caterpillars
he sidesteps a water-trap.
Unhidden by the short grass
he picks his way to tarmac.

Catches scent of female.
Steps over double lines.
Hears accelerating growl.
Is charged at by unblinking eyes.

Instinct curls him instantly, contracts
his muscled back.
Five thousand spines
stand to attention. Waits for the attack.

Road Kill

A magpie has taken a starling chick
Across the road in front of the flats
One that fell struggling to make its first flight.
Now the rest of the gang have come down from the roof
A screaming mob, harrying the magpie
Darting in and out again from walls and fencetops
Scattergun screeches that rip through the air.
It doesn't put the magpie off
It's a heavy-shouldered thug, putting the boot in
And it goes on doing it
Ramming down with its beak
Trying to kill the chick, but it's still alive
Fluttering its wings, mouth gaping.
Such a commotion!
The morning's being wrenched inside out
Sliced open and eviscerated by those cries
And the tangled mass of noise and violence
Scattered across the glistening street.
And now the magpie is moving from foot to foot
Head pushed down and forward over its prey
Swaying, hypnotic – stamp, hop – stamp, hop –
Shiva's life-and-death dance
Turning the world under his heels
As the prayer-wheel hums in his body.
Then stab again, stab, and stab
A relentless hammering
And the screaming won't stop it, the rage
The flapping riot of indignation won't stop it.
This is the way things are.
Stand at the window, let the glass hold your gaze.
This is the staring face behind the mask of beauty
And this is the mask of beauty.

Pica *pica*

They say magpie is cursed
for it wouldn't sing a lullaby
to the crucified Jesus.

They say magpie's a bird of ill omen
for it wouldn't enter two by two.
Stood sentry on the ark's roof.

> *Killer of songbirds!*
> *Wedding ring snatcher!*
> *Harbinger of the Devil!*

I thought it was black and white too
then I looked closer –
saw iridescence of green and blue.

I heard it *chacker chacker*
in large flocks in Spring
yet use soft tones when courting.

> *Killer of pests!*
> *Sower of seed!*
> *Street cleaner!*

Watch it choose select pieces
while judging car's speed
then confidently hop aside.

Watch it assess
with tipped head and bright eye,
or hear it socialise.

See it peer deep into a mirror,
recognise its own reflection but
not be frightened by what it sees there.

Dead Badgers

Three of them on the road down
English beasts

Bundled between the kerb and the hedgerow
Like old clothes tied in a bag and thrown out.

Secret stealers of the night
Come to grief in the shock
And smack of the headlights

And each one a nail driven flush into my head.
It takes me like that

Though I can't explain the sense of loss
Except as a kind of yearning after

A longing that drags me out after dark
Down on hands and knees
For an eye to gaze back out of the deep cave-memory

The animal otherness
The bristle and heat.
But that hole's grown cold

As this one in my skull
The creature long since dug and dragged out

And dropped there to be glanced at as my car swerves past

Into the long, empty distance

Through the bared grin.

Pheasant - the joke

It runs.
Invisible legs - fast
but indecisive.
Head upright.
Body large.
Tail too long.
A Chaplinwalk on speed.

If in long grass
it will bolt straight up
with a clock work whirring
startle itself with a *korr-krak*
seem to realise the physics is wrong
and *a-kok, a-kok, a-kok, a-kok*
attempt to land.

Would it be shocked to hear of the casseroles?
Or the Seasonal game mince?
The Pheasant has spread, bred, and fed by using humans.

a-kok, a-kok, a-kok, a-kok

Who has the last laugh now?

Mating season

Cars pass on blind corners.
Cyclists take on heavy goods vehicles.
Motorbikes speed
well over the limit, and

a pheasant stands
as if in field.
Searches the tarmac.
Looks out for rivals.

To and fro.
This way
That.
This way

Thunk.

Each time you pass
his colours dulled.
Eyes soon pecked out.
Corpse more mangled.

No funeral, no flowers.

The hens he wooed
stand
dumb by the kerb.

A Conjuring of the White Owl

The feather laid across my palm

A blade of light shaved from the moon
The ridged and rippled wavetop from the moon's
Frozen ocean
Where the dead sing
Weightless
Their cold high songs
That thread the ear with a needle of bone.

The stroke of finger will set it flying

A skimmed whisper across the windscreen
A ghost passing
Tree shadow to tree shadow
Making this sudden apparition
As if conjured from a crumpling of fading light
With a cry too high
For the ear's cup to catch
Slicing the glass
Slicing the brain
A diamond clawtrack that opens the soul
To flee in its wake
To flutter

To fall.

Little orphan at the roadside
Little bundle of heat
So soft, so lightweight
Its curled feet

Left to me to cradle in its twilight dying
Stunned by its head-on collision with the world
Watching the eyes film
The gold glaze and dull
Watching the shutters come down
On a gaze straight through to the depths of space

Where the new moon rises

Where the white owl sings.

Rabbit on a roadside verge

A nose. Nudging through
the 'Yorkshire Fog' grass.
Its twitch sucks in trails
sucks in trails, draws
them to nerves.
On into cortex.
In the two-way traffic
of acting, reaction
a message returns.
As safe as you'll know.

A stepping out.
Nose always twitching.
Smells dandelion
smells dandelion.
A tentative approach.
Her ears a-quiver.
Her hind legs slow.
Head down for a moment.
Then blackbird alarm
ear-piercing the traffic.

Brain knows to tell legs
to sit still, *sit still*
while leg muscles tighten.
Ears twisting to listen.
Eyes searching, *eyes searching*.
Nose always twitching.

Her mind races home
to her eight blind babies
in the nest of her fur.

underground

a mole thrusts
upwards and to the side
one forelimb at a time
swims
breast-stroke if the soil is light.

He first digs
shallow, but once he knows
he has no
rivals, down he dives.
Is he unearthing

his lifelong home?
Is he delving towards a family?
He loosens soil
then sweeps
it past his velveteen

coat, somersaults
round, braces his body.
Push up to shafted hole.
Watch the earth erupt.
Trickles out as he turns back.

In the nearby town, rooms fill
with raised voices.
Line drawn on a map. Soon
the thunderous rumble, but for now, in his universe,
it rains worms.

Aten

I

Risen song
A pure, clear note
Struck from skyline to skyline
Across the hedgetops

The night's burst wrappings
Consumed in flame.

Warrior of the morning
Traversing the earth
You drag the world to waking in your flarepath.

The fields are your armies
They send up a clamour of joy as you pass
The sun flies your banner
A bright scattering

And light flashes from the blades of many weapons.

II

With the sun hammered mast-high
Between the spread sails of your wings

With the twisted ropes of the wind taut
To hold you in balance

With the compass point fixed
To its only star

You hang the hook of your gaze
Between the horizons

Hold the world stilled

Hold the motorway embankment
The leathery trees
The clockwork heartbeat of the mouse

Stilled

But for this quivering of wings
At the blade's tip
Poised at the zenith
Before the long slide down

The nirvana of drop.

III

You perch in the rafters
Of your cathedral of evening
Feet gripped to the one remaining wire of light

Slowly loosening itself from the sun.

The rest drifts and crumbles
Across the wide floors of the meadows.

You are listening to the last sounds you will ever hear

Becoming a hieroglyph on the wall of your own tomb
Its treasure scattered among the scavengers.

They have taken it down to the lower world
You are following to find it
Folding the map of the land in your feathers

That ancient parchment, your happy hunting grounds.

You will be gone a long time.
When will you return
With your wings' timbrel

Your risen song.

" To see what is in front of one's nose needs a constant struggle"

      Above Ironbridge

   where cast-iron pillars were dragged
 up
    from fire, fumes, smoke, dust
      to be formed into a resting place,
     I look down
  to the now clear river Severn
   breathe in aromas
      of green and pollen
hear the *er-teach er-teach er-teach er-teach*
   and try to imagine
      that hellish age

    below

 a motorcycle
   screams through gears
     exposes road drone
  flaunts pollution that's been with us since Industrial birth
     is getting worse
  and I am reminded of Orwell's words
which makes me swear
    that nothing will change
    unless I start to.

Lord of the Wood

Today I saw the lord of the wood
Stepping out daintily the paths of his realm
And he was branched with glory, and crowned
With the morning and the dripping light.

He was shadow and he was leaf-shade
He was the riven heart of the oak tree
Whose roots sang themselves through his blood
And he was nameless in his kingdom.

Custom was strong in him, the secrets
Of that neighbourhood were velvet
To his ears. The balance of the year
Was weighed between his shoulder blades.

Today I saw the lord of the wood
I came upon him unawares as his gaze
Struck my moment. And I would weep
For the knowing that was put into my heart.

Red deer stag

Amused with naming
at first -
calfe, brocket, spayard, staggerd -
their king of the wild
is not worthy of man's pursuit
until age has crowned it ten tines over
and it is named as hart.

Hunting *par force*.
The noblest of sports.
The Quest.
The Assembly.
The Relays.
The Unharbouring.
The Chase. The Baying. The Unmaking
and The Curée. Grand words

that camouflage
the expert huntsman's tracking
while drinks are downed
their chatter mounting
the grouping
of the rache, the running hounds
all waiting
while the stealthy lymer
noses out their quarry

then they join
in its running down
horses galloping
hounds bark, men shout
acceleration in pace and sound

to its final moments
when eyes stretched back
its hide lathered in grey sweat
shallow breaths labouring
the moment for its last stand
then hounds commanded
from attack, sword
drawn and passed
to the party's most prominent.
The death

as if it means something
then deer dissected
dogs rewarded
the head a trophy.

Some stories tell
how a stag
can live millennia
and how a bone
that is lodged
in the centre of its heart
protects it from a fear-filled death.
This beast of venery

antlers hewn from ancient forest
with velvet-mossed branches
stands now on misty moorland
holds his head still.
Unwavering vision.

While his harem of hinds
ruminate on heather
he challenges the next rival
by belling and roar call.
They start to walk in parallel.

Autumn Rite

The sound the stags' antlers make as they lock together in a clearing in the wood above the quarry one morning in October –

A hard clattering rattle
With a hollow after-echo
In the wet trees.

The sound of the victorious stag's voice, heard from further down the quarry in the hidden, wooded valley –

Dry, deep, a rasping
Grated booming, as of
Bark cracking
A tree splitting.

The way the herd of does are glimpsed running towards the stag's voice –

A sudden scattered
Flash-fragment through the undergrowth
Quivering of twig-ends as they pass by
Tail-flutter, hoof-tingle
The high-voltage approach.

What other sounds are heard, peripheral to this grand drama –

A woodpecker's rolling
Stuttered laughter, the jay's
Alarm-scream, the dove's wing-clatter
A crow tearing a hole in the sky.

And what is experienced after –

A secret silence
A whisper in the blood
The deep below singing
Of generations.

A Folk Tale

Spikes in his beard
A crown of thorns
The horns of a new moon clamped on his head.

His bite is ice
His diamond-glinted coronation has become a nightmare.

He sends his messengers, the birds
To seek the jewel that will make him live forever.

They fly about fearfully searching under hedgetops
Find only mist-grains, a dead rat
(Though the jewel is hidden in the rat's gut).

Many die of exhaustion and never return.

His bride died of his love

A single embrace that lasted all night.
Now her dawn ghost lifts up and passes slowly
With heavy wingbeats and a frightened eye

And a long neck outstretched like a silent cry.

In his castle of frost
And frozen webs
He is planning the murder of his entire family.

But his own power is working against him
The magic mirror is ruining his face

And already he has become this shabby buzzard
Humped on a branch in the rags of his robe
And the crows are gathering to pick over his bones.

Two Crows

A rainy skyline
Slumped hills
Mist in the trees
A heavy stillness in the leaves

And a dead tree
Where two crows are talking
In fractured light
Beneath the hum of the pylon wires

Shouldering the weather
In the rags of their cloaks
Watchmen at the world's end
Against the day's fall.

The day after

The day after
was a frosty spring morning,
the valleys and dips spilled out mist
while the sky moved from grey to cerulean.
The propagators, though reassuringly warm,
had not yet held their seeds for long,
but the trees were a-twitter
with great tits, a robin
and sparrows hopped along the hedge top
craning their necks,
as I craned back at them. There were drifts
of sheep and higher bleats,
and while I watched
grape hyacinth eggs
with daffodils stood over them, I thought
they're right,
it *is* the time to start anew, and I felt biblical for that moment.

Tears for Achilles

Each one of them I kill
Makes me live a little longer

I

I love killing

It gives me a thrill

A kick like nothing

Else you can name

Like inhaling

That first

Deep breath

Of the morning

With the salt tang

Off the sea-back

Before the heat

Breaks through

So sharp and clean

It makes you glad

You're alive.
    *

There's a joy in it

That's fierce

An absolute freedom

Standing in

The sun's glare

As my shadow

Throws dark

Across the sand's

Remorseless glitter

And my grin

Burns into my face

And into the whole

Shattered landscape.

II

I see men
Who are hardly more
Than boys
Crying for their mothers
I see men
Whose mothers
Are long underground
Crying for their mothers
To come, come quickly
Come now, please come
Mother mother mother
And take the pain away
Their mothers do not come
Only death
Swift or eventual
Takes their pain away.

*

Such as this one
Cradled in my arms
I watch him dying
The colour of his
Skin changing
A pallor flowering
Beneath the sunburn
Feel the heaviness
That suddenly
Weighs in his limbs
Dragging his soul down
Into its underworld
Mine the last
Living face he sees
As I ease my blade
Out of his body
Let him drop, forgotten
And look up, alert.

III

Though no god

Protects me

Though I ask for

No god's help

Or blessing

Though no god's name

Ever taints my speech

And I am under

No god's jurisdiction

Though I have consigned

Every god I ever heard of

To the junkpile

Rubbish heap

And when I approach

All the gods

Slink off whimpering

Inside their rags

Though every man I face

Has been abandoned

By his god

When I kill

I am a god.

*

And this

Is my god's grin

Fixed in its helmet

These are my

Narrowed eyeslits

Aimed along the shaft

To the slick glittered point

And the bared neck

This is my brain

In its bone casing

A scream of nerves

Tied in a knot
These are my feet
Planted at earth's
Exact centre
This - my arm, raised
This - my knee, pushed forward
This - the sky's weight
This - the sun on my back
And this – the one moment
Of poise and balance
Where the world stills
And I am
Made perfect.

Each one of them I kill
Takes away some of the pain.

belonging

Swallow

twists, turns, swoops,

then chats with flight

on a high-wire

of electric.

His mud nest

snuggles

in the barn with bugs, spiders,

rodents, and an owl.

Old farmhouse roof

takes off each night

as bats leave roost,

pass others from the new build attics.

Fox noses road. In day

this verge

will feed the rabbits.

Peregrine

on clock tower

watches

as eyes wide, from mobile hide,

children stare,

they travel light.

The Hare

The hare
As if dropped from air
Was suddenly there
On the road ahead.

It stood
A hare carved from wood
In the shape of a god.
In the morning's light

Its fur burned bright
Ears erect, upright
A holy sight.
I could feel the heat

Of its body, the beat
Of its heart, the fleet-
ness of its feet
The depth-charge of its bone.

Then the sun
Rose like the barrel of a gun
And the hare was gone
Out across the field

With the world
At its heels.
It turned and wheeled
And on the breath of a prayer

Escaped into air.

First published: 12th December 2012 by Fair Acre Press

www.fairacrepress.co.uk

Typeset by Fair Acre Press, Shropshire
Printed in England by Badger Print, Sutton Maddock

The Secret Fox, Road Kill, Dead Badgers, A Conjuring of the White Owl,
Aten, Lord of the Wood, Autumn Rite,
A Folk Tale, Two Crows, Tears for Achilles, The Hare
© David Calcutt   2012

Suburban nights, Pica *pica*, Pheasant-the joke, Mating season, Rabbit on a roadside verge, underground, "To see what is front of one's nose needs a constant struggle", Red deer stag, The day after, belonging, A matter of taste
© Nadia Kingsley   2012

The right of Nadia Kingsley and David Calcutt to be identified as authors of this work has been asserted in accordance with Section 77 of the Copyright, Designs and Patents Act 1988

A copy of this book is available from the British Library

ACKNOWLEDGEMENTS: Poems from this collection first appeared in: BE Magazine, Dance Macabre, Pentameter, Poetry Cornwall, The Canon's Mouth, Wellington Peace Garden, "We're all in this together" anthology.

ISBN 978-0-9568275-1-7

A matter of taste

Take care when retrieving a carcass.
Learn from corpses of other scavengers.

Check for freshness before bagging.
Select bright blood and clear eyes.

Try rat stew or heron bolognese.
Rich in vitamins. Lean. No additives.

Casserole a gull or tawny owl.
Grey squirrel adds to pies a nuttiness.